WEALTH TIPS

WEALTH TIPS

A GUIDE FOR YOUR FINANCIAL JOURNEY IN GOOD OR BAD TIMES

STEPHEN AND MICHELLE ROMAN

To order additional copies of this book, contact:

Xlibris Corporation

1-888-795-4274

www.Xlibris.com

Orders@Xlibris.com

85802

CONTENTS

I dedicate this book to my father, Stephen J. Roman, and Grandpap, John Ferrante, who have taught me that family always comes first.

For my Michelle
A special thanks to my amazing wife for all of her love and support over the years.

Author Bio

My father died unexpectedly, forcing me to educate myself quickly and on my own. I realized that my formal education of a bachelor's degree in civil engineering and a master's degree in engineering management did not make me "money wise." My army career has led me to command 260 soldiers in combat and in garrison. I have been responsible for fifty million dollars of property at one time and have overseen construction projects in excess of two million dollars, but all of these experiences never taught me to be wealthy. This book highlights my experience—financial and professional successes, which cannot be taught in any one class.

Preface

I had given effort to writing a leadership and financial book over a year ago, with little success. Looking back, it was a weak effort that produced six pages of random thoughts. I had a life-changing experience on a reconnaissance mission to Afghanistan. I was preparing for my third one-year deployment and working as an engineer for a brigade combat team in the 82nd Airborne Division. While in Afghanistan, I developed a blood clot in my leg. The pain in my leg was originally thought to be from a strained calf muscle. Later, pieces of that blood clot broke off and went to both of my lungs, and I found myself in a life-threatening situation. Michelle, my wife, was instrumental in my care and recovery; I am still recovering from this event eighteen months later. After surviving my blood clots, I knew God was keeping me around to start living up to my potential and to impact people in a positive way. On that note, I started writing with a purpose.

Purpose of this book

The purpose of this book is to outline how to create wealth through discipline in your family's daily routines and creating a vision of where you are headed in life. This is accomplished through chapters focused on mind-set, mentored experience, understanding your environment, understanding investment vehicles, and application of these investment vehicles. Immediately, you should notice that the beginning of this book focuses not on the mechanics of different types of investments, but first on the mechanics of you. I believe that to be financially successful in life, you must grasp the mind-set, mentorship, and understanding of your environment first. So let's begin.

Chapter 1

Mind-Set

Before you start going down the path to financial success, you need to establish goals. Take time to figure out the goals you would like to achieve. I also believe that you should have goals for your personal life and a specific set for your work life. You should have long-term goals and short-term goals. I consider short-term goals as things that can be accomplished in two to four quarters of performance. A quarter is considered three calendar months in the financial world. A long-term goal can take two or more years to accomplish. It is important to write down your goals. In addition to writing out your goals, you need to refine them, make them specific, and give yourself a deadline. When a goal is clear and concise, it is easier to complete the task. For example, if you were a sales person, you should have a goal to make X amount of sales by an exact date. Once you have determined a set of goals, be sure it is attainable. Don't waste time on a task that you have no intentions of completing. To be sure you are on the right track, review and revise your goals. This should be done at least quarterly; that way you can be sure your timeline is realistic. It is OK to adjust your goals as you go, but a goal should be a challenge.

In addition to personal and work-related goals, you should also have goals with your family. When making household goals, it is important to sit down and discuss them with your spouse or as a family. You both need to agree on the goal before it is written down. These goals should include self-improvement and relationship goals. Include your children and even extended family members in your goals as needed.

Now that you have your goals, you need to memorize them. There are many techniques that can be used to help you memorize your goals. You can type them out and post them in various parts of your house. I have them posted on my bathroom mirror so that I am reminded of them when I first wake up in the morning and before I go to bed at night. When I am bushing my teeth in the morning and night, I am face to face with my goals. Another technique is to write your goals on a note card and keep them attached to the visor on your car. Pull them down and look at them when you are in traffic or when you are waiting. Try to memorize them when you are driving around. This is much more productive than listening to a morning talk show, and this helps get you motivated for the day. I also have a mission statement on the wall in my office that states the goals I expect to accomplish at work. My group goals at work are posted in common areas such as the meeting room and the lunch room. This technique helps you to become accountable for your goals. The point is to remind you multiple times during the day of where you are headed on your road to success.

Goals and mission statements are vital to building the road to success in all that you do. Both are key elements of your visualization of your future worth and direction. Not everything works out the way we want them in life, but I cannot imagine moving down life's path without a direction. That would be the equivalent of trying to complete a land navigation course without a compass. My goals are my life's compass and they keep me moving in the correct direction. I admit that a few folks can navigate the woods without a compass, but those folks are few and far between in the military world. So just like there are very few individuals who can navigate the woods without a compass, I believe there are very few people that can navigate life without goals and achieve their true potential. Positive forward thinking is critical. Dwelling on past mistakes can be like standing in quicksand, where you never feel you will come out on top. Success doesn't happen overnight; you have to accept the principle of delayed gratification. Visualizing what you are working toward in the future keeps your focus when you are feeling the effects of daily sacrifices you're making to get there.

When I write out my goals, I place the longer term goals first. This reminds me of the end state of my supporting goals from the beginning. I then list out my supporting short-term goals. The short-term goals are arranged in order of the nearest date to the farthest date. Both the long-term and short-term supporting goals are arranged in order of priority. The most important is number one and then the other goals follow in importance. Below is an example of this:

Long Term Goals

1. Ensure these are over two years to achieve
2. Order of precedence by date

Short Term Goals

1. Ensure these are less than one year to achieve

2. Order of precedence by date
3. Typically support a long term goal

Check your goals to ensure they meet the following four criteria:

1. The goal is quantifiable
2. The goal has a completion date
3. The goal is obtainable and not an impossible venture
4. The goal is challenging

The key is to use this structure as a base model and later adapt your technique on how to write your goals out as you get used to the idea. Now I will take you through an example I have used for my family goals. My wife and I have been using these techniques for over seven years now, so your starter goals may be at a higher or lower level of attainability. Below is an example of some past personal goals my wife and I believed were challenging but attainable:

> Be a better husband or wife each day
> Be a better leader each day
> Give with an open heart
> Accumulate one million liquid by age 36 years
>
> *May 2012*
> Pay off primary house mortgage
>
> *August 2010*
> Find a position with USACE*
>
> *December 2008*
> $20 a day income**
> $150K liquid***
> $15K emergency account
> $6K business account
> $10K long-term account

Footnotes:
* USACE is the United States Army Corp of Engineers. At that time, I was looking for a broader experience from the U.S. Army.
** This number is the amount of money Michelle and I are working toward earning a day from unearned income, which is money that comes from certificates of deposits, stock dividends, rent, etc., . . .
*** Liquid paper assets are cash or can be moved to cash quickly.

I then take this written contract to myself and my family and print it. I place these printouts in various places in the house, as previously discussed. When memorizing these goals, at a minimum, I recommend you post this document on your bathroom mirror, in your financial book, in your car, on your refrigerator, and in your calendar.

Now that your goals are set and memorized, you need to start to speak them. This becomes a very powerful tool. Begin to speak the goals at least twice a day. The power behind speaking your goals is that when you are speaking them, you are also confirming what is going to happen and you are staying focused on the target. The power of the spoken word is actually found in many versions of the Bible. It is outlined in the Bible in several places by teaching us to guard what we say about others and situations. Other passages outline how much influence and power we have when using only words. So speaking positive goals is a critical thing. Also, I believe one should focus on the importance of planning and working toward the goals you set. Trust in God and your plans will succeed.

Speaking your goals is only a tool in helping you achieve your goals; you still need to put forth the effort. What I say twice a day sounds like this: God, thank you for all of your blessings and for making Michelle and I multimillionaires that achieve our well-planned financial goals through discipline and vision. Thank you for making me a better husband and leader each day, giving with an open heart, achieving $1 million liquid at age 36. Thank you for the $20 a day of unearned income by December, $150K liquid by December, $15K emergency account by December, $6K business account by December, $10K long-term account by December, paying off the house by May 2012, and finding a position at USACE in August 2010.

I form my goals into a prayer because after I pray for my family, I just go straight into what is written above. Also, I believe that without relying on God, you really have nothing. I have been doing this for the last five years and know that it has focused me in my life's personal and financial journey.

It is your turn now:

Long-term goals with dates

1. _____
2. _____
3. _____

Short-term goals with dates

1. _____
2. _____
3. _____

The number of short-term goals will vary depending on how many you think you will need to keep you on track to accomplish your long-term goals. Think of short-term goals as if they were mile markers in a marathon race.

Now that the goals are written out, review them. Did you make them challenging enough? Are you thinking positively about your future? What you expect in life is often what you get. In other words, do not sell yourself short on your goals. Make the goals realistic and challenging, and then go after them. Achieving them will take work and faith as the days pass, so ensure the final destination is a worthy one. Now, take the time to adjust your goals as needed.

Michelle and I created what we called a future book which is stored in our home. Our future book houses all of our family's paper investments, life insurance policies, other insurance policies, real estate statements and values, social security statements, and annual financial reports which are in a history section. In the front of the Roman's future book, I keep paper clippings of the stock market high and low point in the recent years, a federal funds effective rate chart, and a Bible verse.

The first clipping's title is from when the Dow Jones Industrial average pushed over the 14,000 point in 2007. This is the highest level the Dow Jones Industrial average has achieved since being created in 1896. The second clipping is a graph showing the time period of July through October 2008 relating to the DOW. Horizontally, the graph has the time values in days; vertically, it depicts the values from 7,900 to 12,200. The closing value of the DOW is plotted using the closing value each day for two months. What jumps out from the depiction is the loss of just under 3,000 points the DOW experienced during that time period.

I keep the first clipping to always remind me that there will be a peak to everything. Also, that near the peaks greed kicks in and that is where reckless decisions are made. Sometimes these decisions are made on the way up to these peaks and the reasons just haven't been exposed yet. A great example is when many American consumers used the relaxed mortgage loan system in the mid 2000s to borrow funds to live an over extended lifestyle. Examples include borrowing on their home's equity to fund a new boat or other discretionary item. Other individuals used adjustable rate mortgages and were not prepared for the cost of the loan when the rate moved upwards. Companies were packaging this debt again and selling it as more elaborate types of securities. So greed and extreme risk taking on top of people owning securities they did not understand set an unstable foundation. When people began to default on their mortgages, these practices were exposed. The problem was that instead of only one loan defaulting, it caused multiple loans to default at the same time because they were based on the same asset. There are other reasons for the decline, but this one stands out to me.

The second clipping, hightlighting the market drop, shows not only the result of greed but more so the result of fear. Fear can spread similar to a virus in the body. A virus untreated can eventually kill you or cause great harm. During October 2008, I remember people in my unit saying things like, "I am taking what's left out of the market today. Even with a 50% loss" or "I am going to liquidate my Roth IRA and leave that money in a checking account." More and more people began to talk that way and I watched that negative mind-set spread quickly. Many times I urged these people to take a look at the entire history of the DOW before making up their minds. Some people listened to my advice and understood that the market goes up and down, although sometimes drastically, and were able to make educated and not emotional decisions about their money.

What is happening in today's markets has happened before. The underlining reasons may be different but the reaction from the public is nearly identical. To further drive home these points, the following example occurred in the early 1700s. The South Sea Company was a British joint stock company that traded in South America. The company bought a substantial amount of the government's debt, ran a campaign to fuel speculative buying of the stock, loaned funds to the public for the sole purpose of buying the stock, and had corrupt officers running it. Finally, the company could not cover its financial obligations and the South Sea Bubble of 1720 burst, leaving many people in financial ruin. Sir Isaac Newton even made and then lost money by investing in this company. I believe that if you see a large group of people moving in one direction, think twice about it before following the herd.

The third clipping is a graph showing the Federal funds effective rate in comparison to the S&P 500 and Lehman Brothers Aggregate performance over time. The Federal funds effective rate is basically what it costs to borrow money in the United States. If the rate is high, then typically things like mortgage rates and credit card interest rates are high. The S&P 500 is an amalgam of the value of five hundred of the largest domestic companies in the United States which creates a large capitalization benchmark. At that time, the Lehman Brothers Aggregate was a standard benchmark for bond performance. Over twenty-five years, the graph depicts a gradual climb in the Lehman Brother Aggregate and even a greater increase in value in the S&P 500 taken as an average. The Federal funds effective rate goes up and down. On this graph, I wrote in black pen is "inflation—what level." The point I was making to myself is that the stock market, bond market, the rate at which I could borrow money will go up and down over time, but I always have to understand the effect of the unseen monster called inflation. Inflation must always be considered and must not go unnoticed. During the last eight years, inflation has been 3% a year on average. Inflation is the average increase in the cost of products across the economy. One industry or sector may be greatly affected by inflation while another industry or sector is not; overall, it affects you.

The final clipping is a verse from the Bible that reminds me that my strength is derived from God. With God on your side and with hard work, there are not many goals that will be out of your reach. I recommend finding your verse that inspires you to keep working toward your goals and add that to your future book.

So every time I open the Roman future book, I am reminded that the stock market can adjust up or down wildly due to people's fear or greed. The second is that if I am overly conservative the inflation monster will eat any hope of return or possibility the principle investment. Finally, I need to believe in my goals and plan. I encourage you to put a few reminders in the future book you create. They could be newspaper clippings, a quote, or a Bible scripture. Add as many reminders and types of reminders as you need.

Another critical book Michelle and I have created is a dream book. This book helps Michelle and I visualize our amazing future. We take cutouts from different types of media and place them into the future book. These cutouts consist of pictures of items we would like to own in the future or pictures and phrases that help us visualize a concept we would like to implement. Examples of these concepts include home improvement projects or a management technique. Pictures speak a thousand words, so the dream book will definitely help with your visualization. This book is placed directly next to the Roman future book. If you can see yourself at your final destination, it will help you find ways to get there because your goal will become more real to you. So start a future book and dream book for your family today; they're worth it.

Quality time with your family is a corner stone of success. If you are single, this may just be some time alone or with a special friend. The key is to plan it and schedule the time. Some great examples are playing chess or checkers, taking a walk, or taking a beach getaway. Notice how some of these do not cost a cent. Also, another point is that I did not list TV or a movie. The rule of thumb here is that if you are not interacting, then that time is usually not the best quality time. I am not saying that going to a movie is a bad thing to do; it is just that without interaction, I believe your relationship doesn't grow. I believe the drive to and from the beach for me and my wife are the most productive when discussing issues because that is all there is to do. Always plan quality time from one event to the next, meaning that while you are on vacation, think of the next time you are going to go somewhere.

The five major concepts to take away from this chapter include the following:

1. Set your goals
2. Speak your goals
3. Create a future book
4. Create a dream book
5. Ensure you prioritize your quality time

Chapter 2

Mentored Experience

Ever hear the expression experience is the best teacher? A good statement but a better one is a **mentored experience is the best teacher**. Michelle and I have always put extra effort into finding people to talk to that have more life experience, more wealth, more experience in real estate, and more of whatever we are about to venture into.

To go to someone for advice and counsel takes you or the couple to be humble in nature. I will admit, for a male, this can be a pride-swallowing event. This key is to understand the end state. The advice you get and follow may save you thousands of dollars or even a relationship, which you can't put a value on. There is nothing wrong with admitting that you and your spouse do not know everything about life. The Bible repeats this theme of mentorship over and over again. Multiple passages focus on the importance of having a teacher or, in other terms, a mentor. One of the most important decisions you make in life is who you surround yourself with.

The people around you daily could be a good source of counsel. Some examples include that fellow employee that you know that has a real estate business or the other coworker that has a home business. Remember, after you find the right people to talk to, there are many ways to hear what they have to say. For example, you may want to buy them a cup of coffee or dinner. I think the coffee or dinner sit down depends on how much time you think the conversation is going to take. Remember, if you are asking for someone's opinion or how they approached a particular problem, you may not agree with the information you receive. Be careful not to be a Monday morning quarterback. So if someone tells you, "I think you're heading down the wrong path," don't take it the wrong way. A wise person not only listens to counsel but it is more that he loves to receive it. The Bible is packed full of wisdom and there is no other book like it. Countless times, the Bible focuses on the importance of seeking council.

I do believe that before going to someone for counsel, it is your responsibility to educate yourself on the subject matter at hand. Do your homework before you sit down to counsel with someone. They will appreciate educated questions from you.

I highly recommend that you write down questions before you sit down with the person. Always ensure you have a pen and paper for note taking. I always know if someone is in the receive mode when they have a pen and paper. I make it a habit to never talk to a superior without a pen and paper in hand and ready for note taking. People remember none of what they hear, some of what read, and all of what they do.

Some people will go to great lengths and cost in order to receive some quality counsel. These people understand the power of the **mentored experience.** How much would you pay for one counseling session? Of course I am not advocating that all counseling should be paid for by the hour, either. If you are already into investing, the example below will make more sense to you initially. If you do not know who and what Warren Buffet is about, then I encourage you to research his life achievements.

In recent years, Warren Buffet has held a charity auction for anyone who wants to eat lunch with him. One year, a fund manager paid $2.1 million for this prize. Although the proceeds went to a charity, the point of the meeting engagement was the chance to speak to one of the greatest financial minds of our time.

Another way to look at counsel is through a book. Yes, a book can provide great counsel or supplement a mentor's guidance. Everyone should be on a reading program anyways. Throughout my military career, very few leaders have understood this concept and ensured his subordinates were on a reading program. The way a mentor helps in a reading program is that he or she can offer book suggestions based on what your current needs are. Usually, books offer suggested readings in the back of the book, like this book. Please refer to my suggested list of books for your next read or counseling session. As soon as you have completed a book, you should be ready to purchase the next one. I currently alternate reading books with subjects focused on financial, leadership, relationship, and my profession. I read the Bible with my wife daily in order to cover the faith aspect of my life. The Bible has numerous readings that are based on wisdom. This wisdom comes from experiences and teachings from thousands of years ago. I recommend adding the Bible to your reading program if you do not include it currently.

Ensure you rotate the subject of your books. I enjoy the financial books, so that is what I gravitate to when buying a book. When you read, remember you need to walk away with knowledge. When reading books from your reading list, ensure you use a highlighter or take notes. Read as if you were going to take a written test. Besides, your test is life, why not prepare for it the best you can?

A final thought on why I know receiving counsel is so important for everyone regardless of position or title: I believe that God made life a team sport. What I am getting at is that you need people in order to become successful through either leading them, caring for them, or through being a good follower. I do not know of a way to achieve wealth, success, or an overall healthy lifestyle by locking people out. Trust in the Lord and not your self alone and he will guide you to where you need to be. Notice I wrote need to be and not where you want to be. God knows what timing is the best for you; just have faith that your persistence will be awarded.

Overall, the most effective military leaders I have worked for have always approached decision making in what I broke down into four steps. The first step is gathering the facts. The second step is identifying the information gaps. Knowing what information gaps exist allow you to make assumptions. These assumptions allow you to continue on with the decision making process and also highlight the areas you are assuming risk in by not having all the facts. Third, convene with other leaders in order to seek out their point of view or seek higher counsel. Finally, make the decision. Notably, officers that did these steps when I was a lieutenant are the officers that are on their way to be generals. These people always seemed to be the ones who made step three a very deliberate step. Also, these people always stated when they needed more time for counsel in order to make the decision. I believe there is no coincidence that the majority of successful officers I worked with in the past relied on counsel heavily.

There are two critical concepts I hope you take away from this chapter. First, it is up to you to seek out the best advice you can find when making decisions. The second concept is to seek out mentors and develop life-long relationships with them. I truly believe that if you adhere to these two concepts, you will inevitably arrive at your final destination in a shorter time and with fewer struggles.

Chapter 3

Understanding Your Environment

I believe that understanding your environment and the people in it will inevitability result in you having a more successful financial journey through life. I developed the following rules after commanding two companies in the U.S. Army, my life experience, and from just generally watching people. I have added rules over the last ten years. I got the idea from when I was a lieutenant in a basic demolitions course. The instructors had rules of thumb for the uses of explosives. For example, if you wanted to cut steel, use C4, which is a type of explosive. This has to do with the speed it explodes at and the force it creates at the point of explosion. I could always remember this rule of thumb. So in the spirit of keeping things simple, I started to create rules as I dealt with reoccurring themes and situations. As you read these rules, remember that the key to doing well is to understand your environment and to be able to relate to the people in your surroundings.

Rule One:
Everybody wants to feel important.
You need to treat people with the respect that they deserve and take the time to make them feel important. It is as simple as a kind word. Another important approach is to have eye to eye contact. Have you ever tried to have a conversation with a person and they never look at you while you are talking? I have and I always felt as if what I was talking about wasn't important enough to rate their time. This usually left me with a deflated feeling. This is something to consider the next time you are texting on that BlackBerry at eighty words a minute and someone starts talking to you.

When dealing with people in the work environment, always try to be the first one to ask how they are and how their day is going. I ask about something personal such as how their family is or how a task they are working on is going.

Building relationships with people takes effort into knowing who they are. You should always make sure people are properly awarded. In the military, I write awards for soldiers and certificates of achievement. This practice can easily be integrated into any company. A simple certificate in a frame is sufficient. To carry this even further, you can have a photographer at the award ceremony. A digital print can be printed out the next day and framed as a nice keepsake and reminder of a job well done. You have to win the hearts and minds of your team. I have found that in leading people, you only get as far as others will carry you. They have to want to carry you. If people know you care about their well being, they typically will want to carry you to a successful finish. Master rule number one and I guarantee your team will produce supernatural results in comparison to the previous efforts.

Rule Two:
Everybody likes to hear themselves talk.

If you are a leader of any organization, whether it is at work or at home, focus on becoming a master of listening. When you do more of the talking instead of the listening, you end up missing out on important ideas, key issues, or general knowledge that becomes wisdom over time. One key to becoming a master listener is once you are in the listening mode, look the person in the eye and give occasional feedback. I have had occasions when I was truly listening but didn't give a nod or some kind of feedback and the person thought I was not listening. People need to know that you are receiving their input and information. One thing is certain with this rule: a good manager has to be good listeners in order to thrive.

Rule Three:
It's all about money.

Money and having it is sometimes associated with greed or other negative perceptions. I look at wealth as a way to provide options for your family. These options could be paying for your child's higher education or having the ability to give to charity. Let's face it: The majority of life's decisions involve finances in some way—from where you live, to what you drive, and to how much you give away. Fiscal fitness is an important aspect to both a successful business and a successful home life. Productivity at work and at home should always be tied to money in some way. When making financial decisions, you need to quantify it in tangible numbers or value. I recommend getting all of your decisions into a dollar amount whether it is a career move, a task at a job, or just simply saving a little extra money. For example, in the home, when planning to purchase something, always quantify in a dollar amount. You can plan for the money needed and hopefully avoid any unexpected debt.

I think a great exercise is to find out how much federal taxes you pay as a daily number. I leave out the state and local taxes because the federal daily tax is pretty easy to calculate. All you have to do is to take the amount of taxes you paid last year and divide that by three hundred sixty-five. This number will amaze you. I believe this number is a great number to try to overtake in your income per day goal. Of course, this number does not even take into account the taxes you pay on things like your electricity bill. Yes, you do pay taxes on that too.

It is a true statement that if you are paying taxes, you are making money. So the more you make, the more you get taxed. The key to achieving your income per day goal then lies in the nontaxable accounts and paper assets discussed later. I do believe each family should pay their fair share of taxes in order to support all the freedom we have in the United States. Remember that taxes pay for things like new road systems and the annual maintenance costs needed to keep the roads open. If you are not tax conscious at some point, you will take on more than your fair share of the tax load.

Rule Four:
You become who you associate with.
I used to tell this to my soldiers all the time. The trend was the people who got into off duty trouble almost always associated with each other in some way. The fact of the matter is that a group of people can bring you up to their level or, on the other hand, they can bring you down to their level, or lower. Surround yourself with positive people that encourage you. Be very cautious of a negative environment. These negative environments exist in every workplace, family, and school in the world. The key is to identify these negative situations and people that cause them and avoid both. Speaking positively is like charging a battery. The more you charge your battery, the longer your positive outlook will last. My mother always told me that I was a leader and would affect thousands from an early age. I used to think that was funny growing up, but now, looking back, I believe that statement got ingrained in my brain somewhere.

Rule Five:
The more you give, the more you get.
My grandmother asked me a few years ago to start to give to a certain charity monthly besides what I was already tithing to my church. She told me "You'll see the money back plus 10%." I did not question her because I respected her wisdom and knowledge of the Bible. Michelle and I talked about it and started giving to an additional charity. What I found is that first off it made me feel better by giving more. We did not miss the additional money heading to the charity anyways. I never tried to quantify if there was a tangible

increase in return, but I can write that I felt more blessed for doing it. And as discussed earlier, mind-set is more than half the battle in life's financial walk. Think of it this way, you can neither give nor receive with a closed hand. So start opening up your hands.

Rule Six:
Time is priceless

How much is your time worth? This concept is tough to capture sometimes because it deals in an intangible thing. I mean you can not touch time; you can only think about it. Time affects relationships. The ability of money to compound and how you use it speaks volumes on that type of person you are. What are you willing to sacrifice in order to achieve your goals? The advice I can offer you is one word: balance. Balance can be achieved when you focus your energy on the task at hand. The more efficient at tasks you are, the more time you have to focus on other ways to enhance your income or spend quality family time. Recreation time directly relates to your goals in that you need time to recharge. Recharging yourself will result in more efficiency and focus in your day to day activities. This recharging time must be a scheduled event. Recharging time is so important that it should be on your calendar or you will most likely ignore it and become burned out.

In order to achieve a balance, you will have to build a team of experts around you. This depends on your interests and passions. For example, you may not want to be an expert in the tax field. In this case, hire a reliable account in order to get some of your time back. Reliable is the key adjective in that sentence and it may take a few years to find an expert that provides excellent service at a reasonable cost. It took Michelle and I four years and three accountants before we found the correct person for us. Remember to trust people and then verify their work. Basically, you need to have a general understanding of what you are out sourcing. As you go along, ask questions and build your knowledge base so you can do a good common sense check on the cost of the service you are receiving and their final product. Areas that Michelle and I allow experts to manage for us include insurance products, accounting, and property management. I have always enjoyed paper assets so I put energy into that arena, which is enjoyable to me.

Rule Seven:
People make time for what is important to them

You can tell what is important to anyone by how they spend their time. People go through college for four years because they believe that the time is well spent. I remember recommending to soldiers to go to college after work or take one class a week, especially classes in the financial field. Normally, people would say, "I do not have the time" or "maybe later." When walking around the areas I was responsible for weeks later, I would hear the same people telling their exciting weekend stories or even their adventures after work playing video games. The point is I knew these individuals had the potential to make it through college-level courses, but it was not important to them. For example, rule six has recharging time outlined in it, referring to personal or family time. I believe rule seven takes over in that if it is truly important to you, you will make time for it.

Preface two

The following three chapters cover budgeting, baseline financial knowledge, and advanced financial concepts. Budgeting is so important that I devoted the entire chapter to it. I used chapter five to help you create a baseline of knowledge focused on financial concepts and terminology. This will allow you to understand the later chapters in the book. Chapter six focuses on more advanced financial terminology, concepts, and some equations.

Chapter 4

Understanding Investment Vehicles

Part I: Budget

I believe your household budget is one of the most important things you need to grasp in order to be in a good financial standing. The bottom line is that you need to know where your money is going. A way to approach this is a simple Excel spreadsheet or just a hand-written chart. I prefer a printed chart that I fill in the numbers with pen or pencil as the month and year goes by. The things needed include a checkbook ledger and a budget tracker (See Figure 1. Budget tracker). The budget tracker shows what was spent each month. Checkbook ledgers are typically provided by a bank with the checking account. The purpose of the checkbook ledger is to subtract withdraws and add deposits to the account. So really a checkbook ledger could be a notebook, but I prefer the smaller ledger that is the size of my checkbook.

Figure 1. Budget tracker

2010 Payments	JAN	FEB	MAR	APR
Credit Card Pay Online	$0 Type: N/A	$ Type:	$ Type:	$ Type:
Cell phone Draft 28th	$65.50 Type: draft on 28 JAN	$ Type:	$ Type:	$ Type:
Cable Bill Mailed	$90.00 Type: Check	$ Type:	$ Type:	$ Type:
Natural Gas Draft 28th	$47.80 Type: draft on 28 JAN	$ Type:	$ Type:	$ Type:
Water/electric Draft 15th	$60.80 Type: draft on 15 JAN	$ Type:	$ Type:	$ Type:
Mortgage $1,100 Draft 5th	$1,100 Type: draft on 5 JAN	$ Type:	$ Type:	$ Type:
Investment $400 Draft 18th	$400 Type: draft on 18 JAN	$ Type:	$ Type:	$ Type:
Life Insurance. $300 Draft 1st	$300 Type: draft on 1 JAN	$ Type:	$ Type:	$ Type:
Car Insurance $600 Pay Online Semiannual 14 Feb;14 Aug	$0 Type: N/A	$ Type:	$ Type:	$ Type:
Home security $215.40 Bill Mailed Annual March 24	$0 Type: Check	$ Type:	$ Type:	$ Type:
Pest control $240 Bill Mailed Annual Nov 17	$0 Type: Check	$ Type:	$ Type:	$ Type:
Home phone Bill Mailed	$30.10 Type: Check	$ Type:	$ Type:	$ Type:
Savings $450 Draft 19th	$450 Type: draft on 19 JAN	$ Type:	$ Type:	$ Type:
Jewelry Insurance $86 Bill Mailed Annual Sept 15	$0 Type: Check	$ Type:	$ Type:	$ Type:
Charity Check Mailed	$45.00 Type: Check	$ Type:	$ Type:	$ Type:

MAY	JUN	JUL	AUG	SEP	OCT	NOV	DEC
$ Type:	$ Type:	$ Type:	$ Type:	$ Type:	$ Type:	$ Type:	$ Type:
$ Type:	$ Type:	$ Type:	$ Type:	$ Type:	$ Type:	$ Type:	$ Type:
$ Type:	$ Type:	$ Type:	$ Type:	$ Type:	$ Type:	$ Type:	$ Type:
$ Type:	$ Type:	$ Type:	$ Type:	$ Type:	$ Type:	$ Type:	$ Type:
$ Type:	$ Type:	$ Type:	$ Type:	$ Type:	$ Type:	$ Type:	$ Type:
$ Type:	$ Type:	$ Type:	$ Type:	$ Type:	$ Type:	$ Type:	$ Type:
$ Type:	$ Type:	$ Type:	$ Type:	$ Type:	$ Type:	$ Type:	$ Type:
$ Type:	$ Type:	$ Type:	$ Type:	$ Type:	$ Type:	$ Type:	$ Type:
$ Type:	$ Type:	$ Type:	$ Type:	$ Type:	$ Type:	$ Type:	$ Type:
$ Type:	$ Type:	$ Type:	$ Type:	$ Type:	$ Type:	$ Type:	$ Type:
$ Type:	$ Type:	$ Type:	$ Type:	$ Type:	$ Type:	$ Type:	$ Type:
$ Type:	$ Type:	$ Type:	$ Type:	$ Type:	$ Type:	$ Type:	$ Type:
$ Type:	$ Type:	$ Type:	$ Type:	$ Type:	$ Type:	$ Type:	$ Type:
$ Type:	$ Type:	$ Type:	$ Type:	$ Type:	$ Type:	$ Type:	$ Type:
$ Type:	$ Type:	$ Type:	$ Type:	$ Type:	$ Type:	$ Type:	$ Type:

Michelle or I take the values we know will come out of the checking account the following month and subtract these values the last week of the month in a checkbook ledger. We ensure that life insurance, savings, and investment values are subtracted first. As we subtract the values from our checkbook ledger, we write the value in the budget tracker and highlight it. When we get the monthly checking statement from the bank, we check off the values from the budget tracker. So this system is not only a way to discipline your spending habits but also is a great way to check on what is coming out of your account. Notice that the insurance draft is on the 1st, investment draft is on the 18th, savings draft is on the 19th. I get paid twice a month, so I spread withdraws out over the duration of the month. The key is to subtract the amounts from the ledger before the month begins. The subtracted funds become the money you know you cannot spend. The payment column of the spreadsheet has what the payment is for, how the bill will be paid, and when the bill is due. In spreadsheet lingo, a column is vertical and a row is horizontal.

As you figure out where the money is going, ask yourself the following:

Do I pay myself enough?

Sounds like a strange question if you are not already in the habit of ensuring you are paying for your future. These payments should include investments, savings, and life insurance before you start looking at your other bills. These investments should be automatic withdraws each month and should be subtracted before any other expense. Michelle and I have always practiced this technique. The great thing about subtracting these amounts at the beginning of the month is that you know how much money is left after paying for your future.

Your first step is to pay off your credit card. Stop using them! I believe they were created for emergencies only. The second step is to accumulate an emergency account that equals approximately three to four months of your household expenses. Notice here that I do not say three to four months of your pay. Ensure you use your household expenses to calculate the amount needed for your emergency fund.

Writing your expenses down as you spend is the best way to find out what your household expenses total per month. My wife and I put a dry ease board up in the kitchen next to the door from the garage. Seeing the board when we entered our house reminded us to get out our receipts and write down the amounts. You will need to do this for about three or four months. Then just take the average of these amounts to obtain your household expense number. It also makes you accountable for what you have spent because you will clearly see your expenditures.

Overall, a budget is a system of management in your household or business. Saving time takes time; basically take the time up front to set up your system for managing your budget. Having a good system that works for you will save you time later on. For example, set up a folder or basket that each spouse puts their receipts into each day, so at the end of the week, subtracting the receipts from your ledger is easier. This doesn't have to happen every week, so you need to set the frequency you are comfortable with.

Before taking action into other areas of the financial world consisting of paper assets, real estate, and other businesses, you need to accomplish step one: create a budget and step two: save three to four months of your household expenses.

Below shows an example of a household budget outlined in a percentage form. These percents are based off of your take-home pay:

Mortgage = 30%-35%
Living costs for food, car payment, etc., . . . = 35%-40%
Life insurance = 10%
Saving = 10%
Paper investments = 10%

No more than 70% of your income should flow toward the cost of living including mortgages. The other 30% of your income should be used for insurances, investments, and emergency savings. To ensure you stay disciplined to allotting 10% to insurances, investments, and savings, remember the automatic investing concept.

When the money is taken out of your account, you can't spend it. Besides, paying yourself is the best thing you can do. Once you get into the habit of budgeting, like all habits, it is hard to stop.

Chapter 5

Understanding Investment Vehicles

Part II: The Language of Finance

First, I will go over some key definitions I have used frequently in the past decade. I selected definitions I wish I had understood when I was about to graduate college. The definitions are listed into six groups. The six groups include general definitions; tax definitions; organizations and markets of the financial world; bonds & stocks & mutual funds; retirement accounts; and insurance-related terms & concepts. The following definitions in each group are mainly in alphabetical order, although sometimes it made more sense to have some definitions proceed before others regardless of their alphanumeric order.

General Definitions

Annual percentage rate (APR): This is the rate you are being charged in order to borrow money, in a percentage form. Use this number when comparing home mortgages, credit cards, or other loans. APR is also used to define what interest you will receive from a fixed investment. An example of this is a two-year certificate of deposit with at 2% APR.

Annual percentage yield (APY): This is what you are getting paid for an investment. For example, a certificate of deposit (CD) with a value of $1,000 at an APY of 3% over one year means that you will receive $30. How to calculate this is gone over in the next chapter. Keep in mind that taxes are not taken into consideration in this scenario. The takeaway here is that you are earning interest on interest. I believe that when looking at CDs, focus on the APY because you should be planning on holding the CD until it matures.

Asset allocation: This is the amount an individual's financial plan has targeted to be invested in different asset classes. Asset classes consist of stocks, bonds, cash, real estate, precious metals, and commodities. At a minimum, the investor should annually rebalance their portfolio to be in line with the asset allocation plan. The asset allocation plan should take into consideration time, risk tolerance, market outlook, direction of interest rates, amount of money available to invest, and tax consequences. To find your current asset allocation, take your net worth and show it in a percentage form across the asset classes. Basically, take your total net worth and divide it into the value of each asset class you own. The example below shows an asset allocation.

> Cash: 10%
> Stocks: 35%
> Bonds: 20%
> Real estate: 30%
> Commodities: 3%
> Precious metals: 2%

Basis point: 100 basis points equal 1%.

Capital gains distribution: When a mutual fund makes a capital gain by selling a security, the fund passes that gain on to its investors.

Certificate of deposit (CD): This is a paper asset that is guaranteed to produce a contracted APY. CDs have a multitude of durations and require varying amounts of money to start, depending on the issuer. Many of these have penalties if you take the money out before the contracted time is over. Laddering CDs is a good way to take advantage of varying interest rates over time.

Compound interest: When your interest earns interest. APY shows this accumulation in a percentage form. Later in this chapter, I discuss an equation to calculate compounding interest.

Debt-to-equity ratio: This number gives you a quick look into how much debt a company or household is carrying. A high debt-to-equity ratio number means the organization is carrying a large amount of debt. To calculate this ratio; divide the total debt by the total of the asset values. All industries have different average debt-to-equity ratios. When analyzing a stock, look to the industry average for a comparison.

Defined benefit plan: This is also known as a pension, which provides a specific benefit during retirement years. Many government jobs provide these after so many years of service.

Diversification: This refers to spreading out your investment funds into different types of industries or securities within an asset class. Examples of an asset class include stocks, real estate, and precious metals. In the stock asset class, owning international and U.S.-based companies are examples of diversification. Ideally, when a market down turn occurs, all your assets in one asset class will not recoil at once. As Michelle's grandfather says, "Do not put all your money into one thing or with one person." Age, amount of assets, risk tolerance, time horizon, and goals all factor into your diversification plan.

Dividend: This is a way that a company pays a return to investors. These can be taxable or tax free based on the security and type of account the security is in. A stock for example can adjust its dividend at any time; this is usually based on the company's earnings. In a recession, the dividend typically gets cut, so do not solely depend on them.

Laddering: This refers to having multiple maturity dates for a group of CDs or bonds. Structure the ladder so no one CD or bond matures in the same month or year. For example, buy two CDs. One CD matures in one year and the other CD has a two-year maturity length. After the one-year CD has matured, buy a CD with a two-year maturity rate. The interest rates are always fluctuating due to conditions changing in the economy, so you will get different interest rates and the CDs will keep rolling over.

Liquidity: The ability to move any asset to cash. The quicker you can move to cash, the more liquid the investment is. A checking account is very liquid while real estate is on the opposite end of the spectrum, with it not being liquid.

Inflation: This is the rising cost of goods and services. For example, what a dollar bought when you were a teenager is much less now. For about the last ten years, inflation has ranged in the 2% to 3% range each year. This monster will erode your investment if you are not earning more than it, so be mindful of it.

Interest rate: The amount you pay or earn on a principal amount of money. This is expressed in a percentage form typically.

Maturity date: The date the principle investment and final interest payment is due to the bond or certificate of deposit holder. Each type of bond and certificate of deposit has a maturity date.

Portfolio: Starts when you own more than one type of security. For example, stocks, bonds, mutual funds, and real estate.

Prospectus: This is a written document that the mutual fund company, issuing company of stock, or issuing company of another security produces to update share holders and to try to attract new share holders. The prospectus is filed at the Security Exchange Commission (SEC). The thought is that everything in the prospectus is accurate. The prospectus will have balance sheets, usually a summary of how things went in the last year and thoughts on the future outlook. If you are going to invest in anything, you definitely should take the time to read about what is going on with that security. Keep in mind that Bernard Madoff filed with the SEC each year and he managed to run a undetected Ponzi scheme for approximately ten years. Estimates of Mr. Madoff's fraud run currently around $65 billion, which is the largest fraud of record in the history of the United States. A Ponzi scheme basically uses a new investor's money to hide the fact that the manger is not investing the money. The scheme is much more elaborate than that but it gives you the idea. As this investigation goes on, I will be interested in how Mr. Madoff and his partners fooled the SEC and investors.

Qualified accounts: Accounts that offer a tax advantage, either before the money enters the account or after the money leaves the account. An after tax account example is a Roth IRA (pay taxes when the money is earned and not when withdrawn). Before, tax advantage accounts include 401K and traditional IRAs (do not pay taxes when the money is earned only when withdrawn). The thought behind this is that when you are pulling the money out of the account, you are retired or in a lower tax bracket at that time. Growth while the money is in these accounts is tax deferred. There are many rules surrounding these accounts. Please see the IRS guidelines before investing.

Commonalities between Qualified Accounts:

1. Penalties are high if you get the money out of the account before age 59 and 1/2, in most cases.
2. If you take a loss in a qualified account, the loss cannot be counted toward a loss on your end-of-the-year taxes. **This means you should never use this instrument for a speculative investment.**

Nonqualified accounts: Not considered a retirement account from a tax point of view. These accounts are built with after tax dollars, and gains are taxable or nontaxable depending of what paper assets are owned.

Return on investment: ROI is the profit you make on a sale of a security or asset stated in a percentage form. You take the profit made on a sale and then divide that by the initial investment cost. Take that number and multiply by one hundred in order to get it to a percentage.

Yield: The rate of return on an investment.

529 savings plan: The account is designated to pay for future higher education costs for a beneficiary. Earnings in 529 accounts can grow free from federal tax, and withdraws for qualified higher education expenses are free from federal tax as well. You can open a 529 plan for anyone including yourself. You can use the funds for a variety of expenses including tuition, room and board, books, and supplies. The account owner maintains control of the assets in the account and determines the amount and timing of distributions. Account owners can change beneficiaries without penalty as long as the new beneficiary is a member of the previous beneficiary's family. Currently, there are no income limits on this type of plan. State rules on the 529 plans vary ranging from some allowing earnings to grow tax deferred to others not allowing tax deferred growth.

Tax Definitions

Adjusted gross income (AGI): This is the final amount you will be taxed on for any calendar year. For example, add up your earned and unearned income and then subtract any deductions. Unearned income includes interest, dividends, long-term and short-term capital gains, and long-term and short-term capital losses. Deductions may include medical expenses and contributions to qualified retirement accounts. Always use the IRS guidelines which can be found at *http://www.irs.gov.*

Capital loss: This occurs when you lose money in an investment. Similar to the capital gain, there are long-term and short-term losses based on one year of ownership. You can deduct these losses from gains up to $3,000 a year from your income taxes. Also, if you have more than $3,000 in negative losses in a year, the losses can be rolled over to the next year. This concept is discussed later under long-term capital gain.

Capital gain: A capital gain is a realized positive gain when an asset is sold. There are long-term and short-term capital gains.

Long-term capital gain (or loss): A gain or loss in an asset that has been owned for over twelve months. A short-term capital gain or loss is a loss or gain from an asset that is owned less than twelve months. Short-term capital gains are taxed much higher than long-term capital gains. The following example shows stocks being sold, which make a realized loss and gain. The two stocks are in a nonqualified account, such as a trading account, and you sold the two stocks.

>   Stock A makes a gain of $500
>   Stock B makes a loss of $500

Total amount taxed = 0 because there was zero gain. You can carry losses over to the next year as well, although you can only claim up to $3,000 each year. If you have more than $3,000 in losses you can continue to roll over this amount to the next year until it is used up. In paper assets, record keeping is a key. All financial transactions need to have a paper trail. Remember that besides building wealth, you will eventually need to sell some of these assets in order to generate income from them. With this in mind, you need be able to produce the cost at purchase time. Without thorough record keeping, you may be forced to pay more taxes than you have to. For example, if you buy a stock or mutual fund

Year	Share amount	Cost per share ($)	Total Cost ($)
2007	10	20	200
2009	10	25	250
2010	50	22	1,100
2011	30	40	1,200
			Total cost = $2,750

You sell all 100 shares at $55 a share in 2013. So it is a long-term capital gain because all shares are over one year old. The total amount after the sell is $5,500, which is $55 a share times 100 shares.
So what is the gain?
Take $5,500 minus the cost of $2,750 = $2,750.
$2750 is the long-term capital gain.

Imagine if you did not have the records to show the cost at the time of purchase. The Form 1099B for your taxes only would show the $5,500 amount, so you have to prove the reason it should not be taxed at $5,500.

Earned income: Income you make from working for a company. This type of income is reported to the IRS through Form W-2. The Form W-2 is your wage and tax statement. Form 1099-MISC is for miscellaneous income. Some of the income areas this form captures include rents, royalties, and medial and health payments.

Tax bracket: A tax bracket is a range of income taxed at a specific rate. Currently, the bracket includes 10%, 15%, 25%, 28%, 33%, and 35%. For example, if your taxable income was high enough to cross two brackets, you would pay 10% on the amount up to $15,650 and then you would pay 15% on the amount up to $63,700. I pulled an old bracket for married filing jointly off of the IRS Web site in order to show this. The tax brackets change frequently so you should check the most updated version the first quarter of each calendar year. Remember: once you enter a higher tax bracket, the amount you give to the government goes up significantly. Approximately, 47% of all Americans did not pay a cent in federal income tax in 2010.

Figure 2. Tax bracket example for 2006 Schedule Y-1
Married Filing Jointly or Qualifying Widow(er).

If taxable income is over—	But not over—	The tax is:
$0	$15,650	10% of the amount over $0
$15,650	$63,700	$1,565.00 plus 15% of the amount over 15,650
$63,700	$128,500	$8,772.50 plus 25% of the amount over 63,700
$128,500	$195,850	$24,972.50 plus 28% of the amount over 128,500
$195,850	$349,700	$43,830.50 plus 33% of the amount over 195,850
$349,700	No limit	$94,601.00 plus 35% of the amount over 349,700

Go to the IRS Web site in order to get the most update version: *http://www.irs.gov/*. Schedule X is for single status, Schedule Z is for head of household, and Schedule Y-2 is for married filing separate.

Tax exempt: You do not have to pay any income tax on the earnings from the investment. These earnings can be exempted from federal, state, or both.

Unrealized loss: If the security drops below the price you bought it at and you do not sell the security, the loss in value is an unrealized loss.

Unrealized gain: If the investment goes above the price you bought it at and you do not sell the security, the gain in value is an unrealized gain.

Organizations and Markets of the Financial World

Dow Jones Industrial Average (DJIA): This index is created by using the thirty largest U.S.-based companies listed on the New York Stock Exchange. The index is used heavily in the media as a growth indicator for the United States even though the Dow Jones Industrial Average depicts a very narrow view of the economy. I recommend using the S&P 500 for your U.S. company large capitalization growth performance benchmark because it represents a larger picture of what is going on in the market place.

Federal Deposit Insurance Corporation (FDIC): This is a U.S. government policy that insures bank deposits up to $250,000 for individual accounts and $500,000 for joint accounts. If you have more than that, you can use different banks to ensure you are covered. This was created so people would leave their money in the banks and not at home in their closet. I read a story last week that a man is selling a water-tight PVC pipe to be used for burying money. He already sold about four pipes. Although this story is interesting, I feel FDIC is a safe bet. The FDIC rules can be viewed at http://*www.fdic.gov.*

The Financial Industry Regulatory Authority (FINRA): is the place you can look up your financial adviser's history, if he or she has any complaints. The NASD representatives are now called security representatives. FINRA is the largest regulator of securities firms and their employees doing business in the United States. Overall, FINRA focuses on investor protection and education.
For more info, visit *http://www.finra.org*

MSCI EAFE: MSCI EAFE stands for Morgan Stanley Capital International Europe, Australasia, and Far East. This index weights each security based on the respective market capitalizations related to the country the security is based in. For example, the weight of Japan securities is about 26%, France holds 9%, and Australia captures 5%. The weights change each year based on each country's overall capitalization compared to each other. There are variations that break down large to small capitalizations. These variations include the MSCI EAFE Large Cap, MSCI EAFE Mid Cap, and MSCI EAFE Small Cap. The countries that make up this index include New Zealand, Portugal, Austria,

Norway, Denmark, Ireland, Singapore, Greece, Belgium, Finland, Hong Kong, Sweden, Italy, Germany, Spain, Netherlands, Australia, Switzerland, France, Japan, and United Kingdom. Overall, there are many foreign indexes and this is just one example.

NASDAQ: The National Association of Securities Dealers Automated Quotations, which does not have a central trading location like the NYSE and is an electronic stock market.

NASD: National Association of Securities Dealers or NASD did regulate broker dealers and registered representatives. As of July 30, 2007, NASD became the Financial Industry Regulatory Authority (FINRA), which took over the job of regulating.

New York Stock Exchange (NYSE): The oldest traditional exchange in America. People place the trades on this exchange.

Securities and Exchange Commission (SEC): Enforces security laws, regulates the security industry, and works to protect investors from fraud.

Securities Investor Protection Corporation (SIPC): This was created by Congress to ensure that if a brokerage fails and goes bankrupt, the individual investor is covered. Currently, you can be insured up to $500,000; which includes up to $100,000 in cash. If you are investing with a firm, ensure they have SIPC.

S&P 500: This is an index that depicts the performance of 500 of the United States' large capitalization companies. I look to the S&P 500 to gauge the daily market performance.

Standard & Poor's: This is an investment company that rates stocks, bonds, and insurance companies.

Bonds, Stocks, and Mutual Funds

The three ways I conceptualize bonds, stocks, or mutual funds include buy and hold, farming, and foresting. Buy and hold is when I am looking to hold the asset indefinitely. Farming is when I buy the paper asset in order to receive a dividend or interest. I look at this as farming because like crops, there is a somewhat predicable harvest. Foresting is when I am choosing an asset for it is growth potential. Once the asset is grown enough for a profit, I sell it. Similar to when a tree is cut down, the sell is a one time event and one time profit.

Bond: A paper investment which is a debt security issued by a corporation or government. A bond's interest can be tax free or taxable. Basically, you are in a contract with the issuer to receive a specific interest rate over the life of the bond until maturity.

Bond rating: An educated guess if the bond will default or not. Typically, AAA is the highest and the lowest is D. BBB is considered investment grade. Usually a low rating equates to a higher yield. Although you can still invest in bonds below BBB, it becomes the question of risk versus reward.

Municipal bond: These can produce tax-free state, local, federal income, or any combination of the three. A municipal bond or "muni" can produce federal tax-free income, but you may have to pay state income tax on it. A municipal bond typically funds infrastructure projects for the local, state, and federal government. Some project examples include rising funds for a highway, school, or dam. This can be very advantageous for people in the higher tax brackets. The below example shows tax-exempt yields versus taxable yields when considering Federal tax:

Taxable income			Tax exempt rate of 4.00% is approximately a taxable
Single	Joint	Tax rate	equivalent of
$8,026-$32,550	$16,051-$65,100	15%	4.71%
$32,551-$78,850	$65,101-$131,450	25%	5.35%

As you can see above, someone in the 25% tax bracket will earn 0.64% more than the same amount of money invested by someone in the 15% tax bracket.

Stock: Ownership in a company. The company uses the money paid for the stock to grow and ultimately produce a return for the share holder and the company.

Market capitalization: This is the value of a stock. The number can be found by multiplying the current stock price by the current number of outstanding shares. Depending on the source, stocks are usually divided into three size categories: large, mid, and small.

Large-capitalization (large-cap) stock: A company that has a market capitalization of over $10 billion.

Mid-capitalization (mid-cap) stock: A company that has a market capitalization range of $2 billion to $10 billion

Small-capitalization (small-cap) stock: A company that has a market capitalization range of less than $2 billion.

Mutual fund: Takes investor's money and combines the funds in order to buy bonds, stocks, and other investments that are then managed by one person or a team of managers. There can be many costs involved in mutual funds from expense ratios, front load fees, back-end fees, and 12b-1 fees. There are thousands of types of mutual funds from industry specific, ones that focus on specific regions in the world, purely bond, purely stock, and even target date ones. The target date mutual funds have you pick a retirement year and the mutual funds manager adjusts the allocation of the assets to balance the risk. The manager works to reduce risk by lowering exposure to stocks and increasing the assets in cash and bonds as the retirement date approaches. The advantage of mutual funds is an investor can get a diversified investment at low entry cost.

Money market fund: Invests funds in short-term securities in order to allow the money held at the account to have a high liquidity. These are not typically FDIC insured and usually offer a higher rate of return than a checking account. The key takeaway is that a money market account is typically not 100% cash; it is quite the opposite.

Bond fund: This is made up of many bonds and is typically managed by a person or a team of people hired by the mutual fund company. The benefit here is that the price of a share is much less than a bond at face value. For example, instead of purchasing one bond a $1,000, you can purchase a share at let us say $15. You are buying a fraction of many bonds in the end. This helps with diversification; the operating costs of the bond fund needs to be considered.

Index fund: Created to mirror the performance of an index like the S&P 500. These funds are typically not managed funds and have lower than average expanse ratios. The way these funds are not managed is that the fund takes a percentage of each company's stock in a particular segment and maintains that percentage by automatically adjusting as the market adds and loses companies. For example, an S&P 500 index fund will own every stock in the S&P 500 equally weighted. So index funds do not typically have a team of financial analysts looking at balance sheets, just a computer system keeping the ratio in the correct balance.

International fund: Invests in overseas markets, which could consist of bonds, stocks, or a combination of both. The title international usually means that the fund invests in multiple foreign country markets. Like any investment, the investor must read the fund's prospectus in order to see the focus of the fund and the fund manager's approach.

Loaded fund: This refers to the possible front-end or back-end costs of owning a mutual fund. *Always remember: All mutual funds are loaded*. The expense ratio is always present and is a continuous expense of the mutual fund.

Expense ratio: This is the cost of owning a mutual fund. The cost covers all expenses from salaries to marketing the mutual fund. Be aware that there could be fees for entry and to exit the mutual fund. For example, an expense ratio of 1% on $1,000, over one year: $1,000 * 0.01 = $10, so you pay $10 a year to have your money in that mutual fund. Understanding expense ratios will really open your eyes to the cost of investing in mutual funds. The list below represents what I have seen as an average annual expense ratio in the following categories:

Large Growth average expense ratio = 1.20
Mid-Cap-Growth average expense ratio = 1.40
Small Growth average expense ratio = 1.50
Foreign average expense ratio = 1.70
Emerging Markets average expense ratio = 2.00

So as you can see, it is very lucrative to be in the financial business, which earns billions off of just the expense ratio; investors never receive a bill. Of course, these average expense ratios change slightly depending on what source you are using. The other thing I have caught on to is that in the prospectus, there is usually an example of what the cost of owning the fund is based on $1,000. The fine print usually states that the example is for a six-month period. So to get the annual expense, you need to multiply by two.

Nonloaded mutual fund: *Again, every mutual fund is loaded because of the expense ratio. So I believe this is a deceptive marketing term*. This type of mutual fund only carries an expense ratio.

Front-end loaded funds: You pay a fee to invest in the mutual fund from the beginning. The disadvantage is that you lose part of the initial investment which never has a chance to compound. The advantages of these include most mutual fund families decrease the cost of front-end loads as you invest more money and these funds typically have lower annual expense ratios. I have used *http://www.sec.gov* in order to compare funds in the same category with their expenses. This is the Security Exchange Commission website which is a government agency with a mission to protect investors. I have found that getting a comparison to be apples to apples, a meaningful comparison, is very difficult. This formula asks for how many years you are looking to invest for, amount to invest, type of investment, expected rate of return, name of the investment, cost associate with the fund—front load, back-end load, and expense ratio. A back-end load is an expense a mutual fund charges when the money is moved out of the account. After all the data is plugged in, the formula produces the amount that the investment would be worth and the foregone earnings. The foregone earnings are the earning you never see because of a front load or expense ratio. I played around with this calculator using a stock fund at 5% rate of return a year using a front load of 5.75% and expensive ratio of 0.62 compared to another very similar non-loaded stock fund at the 0.99 expensive ratio. I found it to about 20 years for the front-loaded fund to overtake the non-loaded fund. So it is possible for the loaded funds to be more cost effective; it just may take twenty years.

The not-so-funny thing is that I own that loaded fund in the example above; I do not regret investing the money at that time. I do regret not taking the time to truly understand what was going on because I may have made a different decision back then. When I figured this out nine years ago, I called that mutual fund company all upset. I know that poor phone operator thought I was crazy. Also, when I was nineteen years old, I used loaded funds because I did not have sufficient funds to meet the initial lump sum requirements of non-loaded funds. Most non-loaded funds required $3,000 or more to start an account. Although over the last ten years, a few companies have lowered the initial lump sum qualification. In order to run your own mutual fund comparisons, go to *http://www.sec.gov* and use the *Run the SEC Mutual Fund Cost Calculator* or use *http://www.sec.gov/investor/tools/mfcc/mfcc-intsec.htm*. This program requires a JavaScript-enabled browser.

12b-1 fee: This fee is what your mutual fund company gets for marketing and promotion fees. Some of this fee goes to the security representative who sold the security to you. So a mutual fund can have a front load fee, 12b-1 fee, and back-end fee, and can carry an expense ratio. It is easy to see why the mutual fund industry is a billion dollar industry and growing.

Net asset value (NAV): This pertains to a mutual fund's value at any given date. The fund each day takes the total amount of money in the fund minus any expenses and divides that by the number of outstanding shares, to equal the NAV.

Maximum offering price (MOP): The MOP is what you buy when you are purchasing a front-loaded mutual fund. The mutual fund company takes the NAV and then adds the sales charge on to it. A NAV of a mutual fund could be at $100.00 per share and the MOP for the same fund with a 5.75% front loaded will be at $105.75 per share. The MOP price is $5.75 more a share; the extra expense is already rolled into the issue price.

Retirement Accounts

Individual retirement account (IRA): These accounts provide tax incentives for retirement savers. You can have multiple types of assets in these accounts, for example, CDs, stocks, and precious metals. Keep in mind that being up to date with the current year's rules is important because the regulations surrounding these change constantly.

Roth IRA: An account that allows you to invest money into it after you pay federal taxes on your income. The Roth allows you to withdraw money tax free from the account after age 59 and 1/2. There are phase out levels based on your AGI that may prohibit you from being able to contribution to a Roth account. These phase out levels change yearly, so go to the IRS Web site to verify the amount. Currently, Roth IRAs will start to phase out for joint filers with incomes exceeding $166,000 and are not allowed when the income reaches $176,000. For single head of households, the phase out starts at $105,000 and is not allowed when the income level reaches $120,000. The Roth IRA rules allow withdraws for certain life events like buying a house.

Traditional IRAs: An account that allows you place money into the account before income tax is accessed. The idea is that you will withdraw the money when you are in a lower tax bracket after age 59 and 1/2. The Traditional IRA phase out rules for joint filers who are not covered by a retirement plan at work, starts at $166,000 and is no longer allowed at $176,000. For those covered by a retirement plan at work, the phase out starts at $89,000 and is capped at $109,000 for joint filers. Single head of household filers covered by a retirement plan at work start to be phased out at $55,000 and can no longer contribute at $65,000.

For both types of IRAs, you must make withdraws before you are 70 and ½ years old. Overall, a hefty 10% early withdraw penalty applies for both the Roth and Traditional IRAs. The example below shows different types of investments that you can buy in a Roth or Traditional IRA account during the calendar year 2010:

Growth mutual fund - Total amount $2,000
CD at 2% APY, maturity 2 years - Total amount $1,000
Stock Ticker symbol BUD - Total amount $1,000
Stock Ticker symbol OII - Total amount $500
Saving account yield 3% APY - Total amount $500
Total = $5,000

This example is not a recommendation of asset allocation but merely to show that you can purchase many different types of assets with the IRAs. If you sell an asset and make a gain, this gain will be tax differed; if you have a loss, you cannot claim this amount as a loss on your income taxes. If you place over $5,000 in a Roth IRA or Traditional IRA during a calendar year, you will have to pay a penalty on the that extra money and take in out of the account.

401(k): This allows an employee to put money from their salary before taxes into an account. The employer has to set up this account which allows the employee the opportunity to participate in the plan. Similar to a traditional IRA, the money will be taxed after the funds are taken out of the account. The 401(k) funds can be rolled over to a traditional IRA when the employee leaves the job, if that person does not want to leave the money in the account at the previous job. I believe the key here is not to put more than 15% of your funds into the company you are working for, if that option is available. Some programs provide matching contributions incentives and vesting. Limits for 2011 are $16,500 unless you are 50 years old or over, then you can catch up contributions of an additional $5,500.

Matching contribution: This is the amount your employer adds to your retirement account with the company. This is used as a recruiting tool and retention tool. Adding 3% of your total salary to a 401K is an example of this.

Insurance-related Terms and Concepts

First, you have to decide on how much coverage you need if something happens to you. Some basic questions include the following:

How much income is needed to sustain dependants?
Will my children have unpaid education costs?
What debts will need to be repaid?
How will inflation factor into your plan?
Can I use the cash value or loan options as an additional paper asset in the future? Typically, loan options are available in whole life insurance contracts and 401K plans.

Before you read the definitions, I feel it is important to go over my mind set on life insurance. Currently, I use term life insurance to cover any debt I have while I slowly build up my whole life policy portfolio. Eventually, I will no longer need the term policies due to the amount of life insurance I carry with whole life. The best-case scenario is to start buying whole life policies in your twenties and thirties. Buying these whole life policies early on allows you to get a lower premium and gives the cash value time to grow. This is why I recommend that your budget should have 10% allotted to life insurance policies. The life insurance industry is just as complex and profitable as the mutual fund industry. Be very careful of what company you use and ensure you read the fine print of all paper work. After all, a life insurance policy is a legal binding contract between you and the servicing company.

Term life insurance: Provides a death pay out only. This type of coverage is much less expensive than the whole life insurance policies when the insured is younger and is in good health.

Whole life insurance: Provides a death pay out and typically builds cash value in the account. These accounts range in values, terms, and conditions. The cash value that builds is normally tax free when the funds are withdrawn. You can also take a loan from these accounts provided the policy remains in force or, in other words, you continue to pay for the policy. Your cash value will be a tax-free withdraw as long as you do not take out of the policy more than you paid in premiums. Typically, loan or cash value withdraws decrease the life insurance coverage amount by the amount withdrawn. Additional dividends or repaying the loan will bring the life insurance policy back to the previous face value.

Annuity: There are many types and fee structures to these. They can be qualified or nonqualified accounts. Typically, they are insurance products that use after tax dollars in order to produce tax-free income after age 59 and 1/2. A deferred annuity is bought prior to retirement years and is focused on providing income after retirement. Deferred annuities are purchased in lump sum or installation variations. Immediate annuity is a type of annuity that you purchase in a lump sum fashion. Immediate annuities are typically bought when you are ready to begin receiving the income. These have gained in popularity during the recent recession. Like all paper investments, annuities can be expensive to own.

Here are my final thoughts and recommendations in regard to chapter five, the language of finance. At this point, if a definition is a new one to you, go back and reread those definitions again before moving on. For additional information, I recommend the following financial websites:

http://finance.yahoo.com.
http://www.finra.org.
http://www.sec.gov.

These websites are reliable and have search engines. The Yahoo! Finance Website has a calculator section in the Personal Finance page. You can use these calculators to find out how long it will take to pay off a loan or how much money you will receive after taxes on a bonus. Overall, keep in mind that terms and conditions surrounding financial instruments are continuously evolving. At a minimum, I recommend checking for updates to things like qualified accounts each year in order to ensure you are up to date.

Chapter 6

Understanding Investment Vehicles

Part III: Advanced Financial Concepts

The following chapter contains additional definitions and concepts I have used in making my financial decisions over the last eight years. These concepts and equations build on the definitions outlined in chapter five.

Dollar Cost Averaging

Dollar cost averaging is a strategy that ensures you invest regularly. For example, you have an automatic investment monthly of $50 that goes into a mutual fund from your checking account. You invest through all types of market conditions, which helps to take some of the emotion out of the investing during the low and high periods of the market. I have seen many examples of how dollar cost averaging can produce a better return than trying to buy or sell during specific market conditions. Timing the market's tops and bottoms is an impossible task. Overall, I believe that dollar cost averaging is a solid method for investing for the long term.

Efficient Market Theory

The efficient market theory indicates that if investors have all the information needed to make an educated decision about a security, the market will produce prices that represent a true value. Of course, when CEOs lie or the books are cooked, the information people are making decisions off of are incorrect, until the correct information gets out. The efficient market concept has gained more backing since the increase of use of the internet. I believe that fear will always be the elephant in the room with this concept because it will always throw things out of whack, like in the fall of 2008. From October to December of 2008, the equity markets lost 30% to 40% of their values. The free fall started due to a weakening economy and other factors, but in the end, people panicked and started taking their money out of stocks. This hysteria accelerated the downward spiral in the market. I discuss fear and how it relates to equity markets in more detail in the market risk section later in this chapter.

Time Horizons and Tolerances of Risk

When investing, the concept of time and risk go hand in hand. Time horizon is in reference to when you want to be able to use the money. Another way to look at your time horizon is looking at how long you plan on leaving the money untouched or having the funds earmarked for a purpose. Risk revolves around how great the chance is that the investment may be lost. The higher the risk, the greater chance the investment value will fluctuate through different types of market conditions. High risk in most cases correlates to the possibility of above average returns. Low risk normally equates to lower more steady returns. When investing, first earmark the money for when you will need it. This will help narrow your focus to find a suitable investment. The following example gives a quick reference to how different types of investment compare in regard to risk and time horizon. If mutual funds were in this example, they would fall between the bonds and stocks.

Risk types
Low risk = inflation risk, keep principle
Medium risk = default risk, lose interest, partial investment loss
High risk = company failure, loss of investment

Type of investment	Risk level	Time horizon
Cash	Low risk	Short range (1-3 years)
Bonds	Medium risk	Medium range (2-8 years)
Stocks	High risk	Long term (8 or more years)

Time Value of Money

Time value of money is an important concept to grasp. Basically, one dollar today is worth more than a dollar tomorrow due to inflation. So being able to calculate the future worth of an investment will help in determining if that investment is a worthwhile endeavor. The equation below allows you to take the current value of money and figure out the future value of that money at a fixed interest rate. Keep in mind that inflation is not accounted for in the equation. I have seen many variations of this concept over the years, this is how I memorized it:

Future amount of money = Amount of funds x $(1.i)^{NP}$
i = the interest rate the amount of funds will be compounded during the period in decimal form
NP = number of periods the investment is compounded. This needs to be in annual terms.

An example: How much will $1,000 certificate of deposit at 4% APY be worth in two years?

Future amount = ?
Present amount = $1,000
i = 4%
NP = 2 years

Note: APY is the annual percent yield. So this investment is compounded once a year for 2 years.

Future amount = $1,000(1.04)^2$
Future amount = $1,081.60

The financial section of *http://www.yahoo.com* has calculators that do the math for you. This is in case you do not have a calculator that has a power function (^).

Market and Diversification Risk

In order to understand Market risk, one must also have an introduction to diversifiable risk. First, Market risks are effects in the market place caused by things that effect most firms. Examples of this include recessions, high interest rates, changes in government policies, and war. Diversifiable risks are effects focused on companies that make up the market. Examples of diversifiable risk include a company winning a large contract or losing that contract, a company going bankrupt, and another company going through a lawsuit. All these actions are happening daily throughout the various market places. Market and Diversification risk vary depending on the type of holdings in the portfolio. Generally speaking, market risk for a portfolio is at 15% and the diversifiable risk adds another 15% for a total of 30%. Remember this is + or - 30% of the net assets invested. An investor can eliminate the diversifiable risk through investing in more than forty stocks in at least twenty industries. So removing the diversifiable risk would leave the investor with a risk of about 15% in market risk.

The import thing here is the public's fear can completely throw this idea into a tailspin like in the end of 2008. That is when losses were in the 35% to 50% range. Basically both the Diversifiable and Market risks went to the negative side of 30%. Then the general public's fear continued to push further into the negative territory based on banks and large capitalization companies failing. So based on this recent experience, I believe that adding 20% to the overall combined risk of diversifiable and market risk is prudent.

> Market risk = 30%
> Diversifiable risk= 20%
> Total risk = 50%

The reason for the increased market and diversifiable risk is based on how intertwined the world's markets have become. The concept of being able to eliminate the diversifiable risk is still sound, but it is important to understand the increased risk the global market place has created. The concept of the global market place is highlighted by the fact that you can buy shares of a company in Brazil if you really wanted to. But is that country stable politically and economically? Also, the American consumer's consumption rate drives many foreign markets as well. Basically, we are importing and buying their products more and more. So if the United States is in a recession, most likely the majority of foreign market will be down as well. **Mutual funds are a great way to truncate diversifiable risk.**

The two largest takeaways include the following:

1. When investing in stocks, remove diversifiable risk through owning at least twenty industries and over forty stocks spread out in those industries.
2. Be prepared for a 50% drop in value because it can happen.

Remember, "Past history does not guarantee future results." This statement can be found in the fine print of many financial statements. Ensure you allocate funds outside of stocks and be ready for market corrections.

Market Cycles

The bulls and the bears is a phase you hear quite often in the financial world. A bear market is an overall downturn in the equity market due to a low-performing economy. A bull market is an economy that supports an overall rising market. No stock will have an all time high every day. To be a great investor, I believe the key is grasping the length of time you may have to endure a down market period. Money in stocks should be funds not needed for fifteen years or more. This is the safe way to account for the possibility of a long down turn, although the downturn could be a much longer time period. The Dow Jones Industrial average went from 14,066 on October 1, 2007, to 8,451 on October 10, 2008, just over one year later. When this was happening, did you think, "Am I really a long-term investor?" One only has to look into the past to find other times that volatility filled the market place. One extreme example of this is it took the financial market twenty plus years to recover from the DOW Jones Industrial high set on July 1, 1929.

The Rule of 72

This rule allows you to divide any interest rate into 72 and the answer will be the amount of time it takes for a sum of money to double.

> Example: A 10% interest rate will take 7.2 years to double.
> 72/(interest rate in the percent form) = number of years to double
> 72/10 = 7.2 years to double
> This equation is easy to remember and apply.

In closing, the basic financial definitions previously listed in chapter five along with the concepts discussed in this chapter are intended not only to give you a baseline of knowledge but are to help you make well-informed financial decisions. I hope that you use chapter five and six to refer back to when faced with future financial planning and decisions.

Chapter 7

Real Estate

This was a topic I was always interested in but never really understood in college. I sought advice and wisdom from people who were financially free through real estate. In the mind-set that successful people always seek mentored experiences, I ensured I learned from someone who not only had done it, but did it well. I counseled with this self-made real estate millionaire multiple times over the last ten years. I created some rules of thumb for real estate based on these counseling sessions and my experiences.

Rule one:
Borrow less than 35% of your income.
My real estate mentor said "borrow as much as you can afford." Always use someone else's money (investor or bank) to control an asset while getting all of the tax benefits. When in the market for a primary residence, you need to determine that you can afford the home. First, determine your budget and figure the amount of outflow you can afford for a mortgage payment. For a moment, I will digress to a concept earlier in the book. The foundation of this decision making process is that you have and understand your budget. You will need that expense number which is less than 35% of your income. The 35% number should include the cost of principle, interest, private mortgage insurance (PMI), home owners insurance, and home owners association (HOA) fees. PMI is an additional cost the mortgage company adds to your loan due to the borrower not putting enough money down on the home. The mortgage companies look for you to have a down payment of about 20% of the value of the house. Anything less than 20% will most likely result in PMI being charged. The monthly PMI fee is charged because the loan company considers the lack of a sufficient down payment a risk. PMI typically gets turned off after the loan is 20% paid off. Loan to value refers to the amount

of equity or cash the borrower has in the asset they are trying to finance. So you may hear something like, "You did not achieve the loan to value needed to avoid PMI." I believe if you are going to end up paying for PMI, you should not be purchasing a house. PMI needs to be viewed as a wasted expense. HOA is an expense that everyone who owns a home in a community pays. These HOA fees are normally applied to community expenses like grounds keeping, security guards, and street lights. These fees can be hefty depending on the location of the house. Thorough research in the beginning will help you to avoid heart ache later on.

Rule two:
Use a decision matrix spreadsheet

A decision matrix spreadsheet helps to take some of the emotions out of the buying experience. You select categories to evaluate the house and then weight each category. When you weight each category, you are assigning an importance level to it. When weighting each category, I recommended assigning a decimal value to each. The weights have to total 1 when you are completed.

For example:

Color of house = .5
Size of house = .5
Total= 1

After the categories and weights are finalized, the next step is to score categories. I recommend using a scoring system from one to five. After you have scored each category, multiply that score by the weight of the category. Finally, total all the weighted scores. Do this process with multiple houses and the highest score wins. Ideally, the categories and weights have to be decided on before you start looking for the house. If buying with another person, the weights and categories must be a joint decision. Figures 3 through Figure 8 show an example of a decision matrix spreadsheet Michelle and I used when buying our first house. We used the following matrix on all properties visited and the property with the highest number is the property we purchased.

Figure 3. Decision matrix spreadsheet example for a house

		Weight	Score (1 to 5)	Weighted score
Distance to Stephen's work		0.2	4	0.80
Distance to Michelle's work		0.2	5	1.00
Cost		0.3	1	0.30
Appeal		0.15	3.5	0.53
Neighborhood (secure)		0.1	4	0.40
School District		0.05	4	0.20
	Total =	1	Total =	3.23

Figure 4. Distance to work ratings

Distance to Michelle and Stephen's work
5 < 10 minutes
4 = 11 - 20 minutes
3 = 21 - 30 minutes
2 = 31 - 40 minutes
1 > 41 minutes

Figure 5. Cost of house ratings

Cost of house
5 < $115,000
4 = $115,001-$125,000
3 = $125,001-$135,000
2 = $135,001-$145,000
1 > $145,001

Figure 6. Appeal of house ratings

Appeal of house
5 = Love the house
4
3 = Think the house is OK
2
1 = We'll live with it

Figure 7. Neighborhood security rating

Neighborhood (secure)
5 = Gated or Guard on duty
4
3 = Home Security System
2
1 = Afraid

Figure 8. School district rating

School District
5 = Best in area
4
3 = Middle of the road
2
1 = Worst

You can apply this concept to any decision. The decision matrix spreadsheet forces you to analyze the venture you are thinking about. The process ultimately helps you produce a well thought through decision.

Rule three:
Debt-to-equity ratio
This ratio helps you get a snapshot of how leveraged you will become after buying the house when using a mortgage. Controlling an asset with someone else's money can work to your advantage. I believe you have to take a holistic view of your finances to understand how leveraged you will become by taking on a mortgage. This provides another check in your decision making process and will ensure you are not taking on too much debt.

Debt-to-equity ratio = debt divided by total assets
This number should be under 0.40
Example:

Assets:
House value = $160,000
Emergency account = $15,000
Investment all accounts = $30,000

Value of belongings (include vehicles) = $120,000
Cash value life insurance = $6,000

Liabilities:

Amount owed on the house = ($128,000)
School loan = ($18,000)
Car loan = ($15,000)

Debt-to-equity ratio = (Total liabilities/Total assets) = number below 0.40
Total liabilities = ($128,000) + ($18,000) + ($15,000) = $161,000
Total assets = $160,000 + $15,000 + $30,000 + $120,000 + $6,000 = $331,000
Debt-to-equity ratio = 161,000/331,000 = 0.486
You did not pass this test because you are not below 0.4 in your debt-to-equity ratio.

Rule four:
Location is everything

Finding your location is probably one of the most important aspects of your purchase. Things to look for are how far away you are from major highways, airports, grocery stores, work, and other services. One important aspect that Michelle and I underestimated on our first house is the value of being in a good school district. Being in the best school district is a huge benefit. You even need to look at where the property is located within the actual community. Is it on a cul-de-sac, is it a corner lot, or in the middle of the street? Is it easily accessible? Ensure you drive the route to work at the actual times you would leave for work. Traffic volume can be drastically different throughout the day. Drive the neighborhood at different times of the day and weekend if possible. You may pick up on things that deter you, like stadium lights on a baseball field next to the house. I remember that real estate agent saying, "Those lights are only on a few times a year." Later, Michelle and I discovered that these lights are on every night for the majority of the year. Fortunately, we did not buy that property.

Rule five:
Buy midrange in value

Buy a home somewhere in the midrange of what homes are going for in that specific neighborhood. You don't want to own the cheapest house just as much as you don't want to own the most expensive house in the neighborhood. The midrange houses are the ones that will appreciate the most. If you are buying new construction in a sellers market, you are going to pay asking price which is determined by the square footage. New construction also means you must determine what you need to add to the house to make it livable. These items may include major appliances, blinds, and landscaping costs. These costs can add up quickly to be over $5,000. If all of that money is not in your budget, then you need to prioritize these purchases and projects. Again, don't forget all of the closing fees needed for the actual sale. Your real estate agent and your mortgage lender can give you an itemized list of all the costs needed at the closing before the actual date.

Rule six:
Understand the tax advantages

The typical rule of thumb to calculate what your annual percentage rate (APR) of your mortgage is after taxes is to subtract 1% from that APR. This is what I call your "actual APR." For example: If your mortgage rate is 5%, you are really borrowing the money at 4% because you are able to deduct the interest paid on the loan from your annual income. Of course, you have to be itemizing on your taxes to take advantage of this.

Rule seven:
Diversify your real estate portfolio

Once you have bought your first house and have learned the ins and outs of homeownership along with mortgages, you will be ready to make your next purchase. Of course, the first step is the budget. Can you afford this venture? After the budget is worked out, this next property can be a vacation home or an investment property. Michelle and I had a huge learning curve when we bought our first house. We learned as much as possible about closing costs and borrowing money. We ended up spending thousands less in closing costs on our second home just because we knew how to negotiate with the lender. **There is no shame in trying to get a better deal**, so negotiate.

When looking for an investment property, ensure the average growth rate in that area is weighted heavily in your decision matrix spreadsheet. Finding the growth rate is relatively easy with the aid of the internet. You can use *http:// www.yahoo.com* that has a real estate link which includes the growth rates of most areas. Growth rates are discussed in further detail in chapter nine. The real estate market is a local market, meaning that the values are driven by what similar real estate is selling for locally. Owning real estate in multiple areas will help to diversify your real estate asset class. To truly diversify, the properties need to be located in different counties.

Chapter 8

Your Occupation and Your Business

Employment/Self—Employment

The bottom line here is that you are trading time for money. Yes, you use your skills and other attributes to accomplish the daily tasks but still you are constantly giving up your time. I believe that these types of income are great but ensure you are committed to creating other income sources. In self employment, typically you are making more money but you spend more time working. As you gain in position, you gain in responsibility and the more time you end up trading to get the desired result. As you trade more time, you give up more energy. You can often feel mentally and physically exhausted after a day of work. This goes back to understanding your environment and also yourself. Work toward becoming more efficient at work. Start to apply your freed up brain power and energy toward efforts to create additional income streams daily. These efforts can be twenty to thirty minutes a day, or much more. It all depends on how quickly you want to get to the end state of achieving your dreams. Remember that creating additional income streams will not happen without effort and time. This is why planning is so important, beginning with a dream which then ties into the goals.

Your business

As you read this section, think of what kind of business venture would suit you. The intent of this section is merely to get you thinking of all the possibilities to bring out your talents in a form of a business, your business.

Currently you are either in school, an employee, an owner of a business, wealthy and live off of investments, or received income from a business system or systems. By being an employee only, you will most likely never be financially free. The employee only way of life is made additionally difficult because you have little to no tax advantages. Business ownership most often requires great risk and time committed to doing the venture. For a business to work properly, you need be there overseeing the operations of it daily. One positive for business ownership is that it does have many tax advantages associated with it. Creating income through investing is difficult because it takes a large quantity of money that the majority of people just do not have. Think of it this way, $1 million in a 5% CD will produce $50,000 a year of income before taxes. Taxes on unearned income can be brutal if not managed properly. A business system creates an income stream without trading your time for that income. The business system receives the tax benefits just like business ownership. I define system as anything you do not have to oversee the operations of daily.

Michelle and I were introduced to the business system concept through an internet-based business system. We started an internet-based business system that sold goods online. The goods ranged from clothes to household essentials. The revenue we made was produced from the commission for each transaction. The commission of each transaction was really the advertisement cost that the company never spent because Michelle and I were the "advisors." My duty in the military made continuing this business system difficult due to rank and the numerous deployments. The bottom line is that this business system never worked for me. At first I felt like a failure when I wasn't making the business work to a high level, and then I realized that I learned many important lessons through my first business system venture. Always remember a failure is a failure only when you do not take away and apply lessons learned. Finding a business system that works for you will take research and possibly a few tries.

Michelle and I then turned to investment property. The keys to this investment property are that Michelle and I do not spend time advertising and managing it. We let a property management company do those things for us. By outsourcing the advertising and management, we are not trading our time for the money. The key is not directly overseeing the daily business transactions while still producing revenue. Things we do with the property include writing the interest paid on the mortgage off of our yearly taxes and keeping records of expenses for our accountant. We invested over 20% of the value of the home into the house because we know that the rent would not cover the mortgage. So understanding the expenses are a vital part to using this method. Also, we avoided private mortgage insurance, PMI, which is a wasted expense to an investor. Another advantage is that we are able to depreciate the value of the home and the furniture inside. The first thing you will need to do is let six months of expenses accrue in an account as the rent checks accumulate. This rental is one way Michelle and I work to keep our money in the family. This is where a reliable accountant can be an asset to you. As long as you keep organized records throughout the year, the accountant can complete the tax return and provide that mentored experience for you.

Michelle's grandpap says, "People do not take care of what they do not own." He is one hundred percent correct in that statement though I believe that you can put measures into effect that level the playing field. One measure is your property management company should have a well-written user agreement. This is a document you must read and understand. The second thing is you need to check on the property yourself periodically, which provides quality assurance. Since checking on the property is a business trip the expenses will most likely be able to be written off as well.

The home-based business is another way to help you keep your money. You can designate one room in your primary residence for your operations. This allows the room square footage to be a tax advantage. Also, some household expenses can be considered additional business expenses as well. Use an accountant to ensure you are meeting the requirements set by tax law. Remember that using subject matter experts is essential. I truly believe there is a business out there that suits you, just start exploring the possibilities. **The key thing to take away is you have to find ways to create income streams that do not require you to be there.** Trading time for money is a one for one trade regardless of your income level. You cannot change time but you can duplicate your efforts. When you create income streams from investing and business systems, you cease having a one-to-one trade and put time back on your side.

Chapter 9

Application of Investment Vehicles

This chapter will not pay dividends to you if you haven't studied the previous chapters. I wrote the word studied because some of these definitions and concepts do not go from pure data to knowledge without truly thinking about them. Remember that life's financial journey is made up of tests that happen every day, and overall it adds up to be one of the largest tests you will partake in.

Recommended Steps: Budget

This concept has already been covered earlier with a recommended approach. This concept appears three different times throughout the book because it is that important. A budget is to building wealth like a dream is to goal planning.

Below shows an example of a budget outline discussed earlier:

Mortgage = 30%-35%
Living costs - Food, car payment, etc., . . . = 35%-40%
Insurance = 10%
Saving = 10%
Paper investments = 10%

Use the format in the earlier example, Figure 1. Budget tracker. If you are just getting used to budget tracking, do it with pen and paper. I really believe this makes you think about what you spent as you write the receipt amount in the ledger. Another key to it is to take turns who does the budget entries during a month if you are married. This allows both people to understand how the budget system works. The other advantage of this is that when you enter an expense, it reminds the person of what was bought and if it a frugal purchase. Also, this sets that person up for success if the primary budget keeper of the house is deployed or no longer there. Many deployments and my father's untimely death taught me this lesson.

Recommended Steps: Paper Assets

There have been many studies that focus on people who win the lottery and seem to have their family's financial future secure. Turns out that most never keep that money and end up where they started from or are bankrupt. I believe this has to do with the person not understanding the concepts of mind-set, mentorship, and their environment. People cannot and do not change overnight. They may have the money but they haven't changed their habits or understanding on how to make that money work for them.

A concept found in the Bible is that money received quickly usually disappears quickly. On the other hand, money saved slowly over time grows. Ensure before taking any actions outlined below that you first have a plan and understand the previous concepts in the book.

After you have your goals written out and a planned budget, do the following steps:

Step 1: **Pay off your credit cards**
Step 2: Create an emergency account
Step 3: Fund your 401K up until matching amount (if eligible)
Step 4: Pay off debt that is not tax deductable
Step 5: Start Roth IRA (if eligible)
Step 6: Start life insurance
Step 7: Start a house down payment account
Step 8: Max 401K plans
Step 9: Save half of each pay raise or bonus
Step 10: Start a 529 (if needed)

Step 1:
Pay your credit cards off. There is no tax credit for paying the interest on these cards, so pay these off first. No matter the size of the debt you face, the key is to face it. Put action behind your plan to start paying off your debt, today.

Step 2:
Create an emergency account that equals approximately—three to four months of your monthly budget.

Step 3:

Fund your 401K up to the employer matching amount. For example, if your employer will match up to 2% and you put in 2% of your pay, the employer will give you an amount equal to 2%. This is an easy gain and you should take advantage of it. You are held to whatever investment options are in the plan your employer has decided to go with. A key point of understanding is that when you leave the job, you can roll the asset over into a traditional IRA if you want.

The rollover is a key part of these accounts because I believe it will be critical to consolidate your assets into one firm or area in order to make your life easier as you approach retirement or when your assets grow to the level that you need help managing them. This is because the traditional IRA and 401K have pretaxed dollars in it. Another thing to consider is that your employer may also have a vesting plan that ties to profit sharing or the matching amounts in your 401K. Vesting plans are designed to entice people to work for the company for longer. Basically, the longer you work at the company, the higher percentage you are able to take when leaving the company. For example, a 25% step plan with a two-year lag could be one scenario. After three years of employment, you would be 25% vested into these accounts. After six years, you would be 100% vested into the plans and be able to take 100% of the money in the account when you leave.

Step 4:

Ensure any school loans or other nontax advantageous debt instruments are paid off. The pay off dates should be included as one of your goals.

Step 5:

After accomplishing steps one through four, start a Roth IRA. Currently, $5,000 is the amount allowed per person to contribute in a year. The main reason the Roth IRA is step five is that you cannot replace the time needed for your money to grow, tax free deferred. Time with compounding interest that is tax free is your ally.

Step 6:

Buying life insurance coverage for your family is a wise thing to do. I recommend starting a whole life policy and a term policy. Starting a whole life insurance policy when you are younger is important because the rates are much lower and the cash value has time to accumulate. Also, there are policies that offer provisions that allow you to increase the amount of coverage at a later date without medical exams. I recommend also having a term policy because you can get a significant amount of coverage at a low cost. The term life policy death benefit should cover at a minimum any outstanding debt you have. Over the years, you should increase your whole life policies to replace the term life policies. I believe the whole life policies then become an asset in your portfolio. Since the whole life policies have so many variations, Michelle and I use an expert in this area in order to save time and research the best plans for us.

Step 7:

Start a nonqualified account that is tax sensible. This will provide you some additional flexibility and this account will be your house down payment account. Remember to only buy a house when you have a down payment that excludes you from PMI. This amount to exclude a PMI payment is normally around 20% of the value of the house. Also, ensure you increase the amount in your emergency account to include three to four months of your projected mortgage payment. When these requirements in step seven are met, use the steps in the real estate chapter to help you purchase your home.

Step 8:

Max out your 401K plan to the current year limit. The current rule in 2011 is that you can contribute up to $16,500 to your 401K plan. The $16,500 does not include the match amount for your employer. Take advantage of this chance to lower your income tax.

Step 9:

Ensure you save half of each pay raise or bonus. For pay raises, plan ahead and make it an automatic deposit increase when the pay raise starts to come into your account. I recommend this because you do not want to get used to receiving the money; besides, you have been living without it anyways.

Step 10:

Depending on when your children will be ready for college, starting a 529 plan may make sense. With the cost of higher education headed upward, saving early is critical.

As you expand the different types of accounts you invest in, ensure that when you look at your asset allocation you include all of the accounts. Do what allows you sleep at night in the end.

Recommended Steps: Real Estate

I believe using leverage is a key to building wealth, but I also understand that each day is a gift. Do not borrow so much money that you worry about it every day, distracting you from your life experiences. That is why step one is important to adhere to.

Step one: Know your 35% expense number
Step two: Create a decision matrix spreadsheet
Step three: Debt-to-equity ratio check
Step four: Start your property hunt
Step five: Complete your offer
Step six: Understand the tax advantages
Step seven: Diversify your real estate portfolio

Step one:

Know the 35% expense number from your budget before you start looking for a property. This number is all inclusive including mortgage, taxes, HOA, and insurances. Once you have a mortgage, you are stuck with it good or bad.

Step two:

Craft a decision matrix spreadsheet with your categories or, if you are married, categories that you and your spouse agreed on. Ensure the weights to each category in the matrix are finalized before starting the house search. Include categories that capture specific criteria that you are looking for in the house. Examples include three bathrooms, hard woods, and a finished bonus room. The one category to add to your spreadsheet is growth rate. Weigh this as heavy as you deem necessary. The growth rate can be found on the Yahoo! Real Estate Website or you can calculate it. All you have to do is take a house with the parameters you are looking for and find what it sold for four years ago and then find what a similar house sold for in the same area at present day. You take the difference in values and divide it by the original sale price. Then you take that number and divide it by the number of years and multiple by 100%, which in this case is four years.

Example: House in 2004 sold for $100,000

Similar house in the same area in 2008 sold for $120,000

1. $120,000-$100,000 = $20,000
2. $20,000/$100,000 = 0.20
3. 0.2/4 = 0.05
4. 0.05*100% = 5% growth rate

Michelle and I used the growth rate category in our decision matrix spreadsheet for a property and it has increased in value every year, even in the current down real estate market. We did not use this category in a different property purchase and we bought strictly on emotion. The property value has gone down every year since the purchase. See figure 3. Decision matrix spreadsheet for a house in chapter seven for an example.

Step three:

Debt-to-equity ratio = debt divided by total assets

This number should be under 0.40, if not you need to increase your down payment or find another house.

Step four:

Start your property hunt. This hunt should be conducted using all means of media available. A real estate agent can be a great asset when looking in an unknown area. The focus when you are looking at a property is to answer the question in your decision matrix spreadsheet. I suggest bringing your spreadsheet to the different houses and answering as many questions as possible while on the site. After you look at more than two houses in one day, you will start to mix up the details. During your property hunt, remember rule four from chapter seven, location is everything.

Step five:

Once a house is selected from the results of your spreadsheet, it is time to figure out a reasonable offer. Remember that an offer on a house is a legal binding document, so bid wisely. Your real estate agent should be your sounding board for the offer as well.

This five-step system works for both primary residences and investment properties. The big difference is in the categories of the decision matrix spreadsheet. In a rental property, ensuring you are making enough to cover the mortgage and other expenses is vital. I recommend using local magazines and a real estate agent to find out what the rent rates are in the area. The next biggest thing to find out is if the houses are vacant or renting in the area. If the market is saturated with vacate rentals, you may have to reconsider. In an investment property, the growth rate of the property should be weighted heavily. I recommend at least 0.4 or 40% of the total decision. In this step, reflect on chapter seven's rule five which states to buy midrange in value in the neighborhood.

Step six:

Understanding real estate tax advantages will ensure you are receiving the maximum tax benefit allowed by law. You may need to consider consulting with an accountant.

Step seven:

Once you master steps one through six, you can look at the option of diversifying your real estate portfolio.

Recommended Steps: Self Employment /Employment

Apply the rules of understanding your environment in order to produce more at your work place.

Rule one: Everybody wants to feel important
Rule two: Everybody likes to hear themselves talk
Rule three: It's all about money
Rule four: You become who you associate with
Rule five: The more you give the more you get
Rule six: Time is priceless
Rule seven: People make time for what is important to them

If you apply these rules, I believe they will assist you in becoming a better asset at your work place. Ensure you work on additional income streams, but be cautious of underperforming at your current position while perusing these ventures. This can be as simple as increasing your knowledge of paper assets through a reading program focused on how to invest. The key is to set time aside daily to improve your knowledge, make a trade, or work on that next investment property. Wouldn't your work take on a different tone if you where financially secure or on your way there? I believe how fast you get to that point depends on not only what you do at work but even more so on what you do after work.

Recommended Steps: Other Businesses

The key point here is to recognize that successful people understand that failing at a task does not equate to being a failure. You must learn from your experiences and apply lessons learned to start that venture over again or to start one that suits you better.

Step one: Find your passion
Step two: Create a business plan that is realistic
Step three: Understand the taxes
Step four: Find a person that is successful in the business you are
    looking to start
Step five: Start

Step one:
Find your passion, in or outside of your current occupation. You may be a civil engineer that enjoys the financial aspect of life or a teacher that loves

to bake. You have a talent or interest that will drive you; you just have to identify it.

Step two:

Create a business plan that is realistic. Who are you marketing to? What does your service or product aim to accomplish? Write these things out and it will give you focus on what you are working toward. You cannot move on to the next step until these two questions are answered. For example, I had a difficult time writing this book until Michelle suggested I work on the purpose of the book more. I refined the purpose of the book and my thoughts became more focused, which made writing much easier.

This business plan must have a timeline for when you envision specific actions to take place. You have to hold yourself accountable to these dates in order for the plan to work. I suggest making this timeline first because then you will be able to envision yourself doing the actions and start to create a positive outlook. Depending on what type of venture it is, ensure you have alternate plans for when things do not go smoothly. Every plan I had as a staff officer or commander in war had to be adjusted upon first contact. The thing to understand is that first contact wasn't necessarily an enemy combatant force. First contact was normally the equipment broke down, the weather conditions changed, or the materials we were promised never arrived. I noticed that whether deployed or not in the Unites States, the first contact phenomenon occurs, forcing an adjustment to the plan. I believe that plans are meant to create a direction for yourself or organization not to be an unchangeable blueprint. In other words, an initial plan is suppose to be adjusted.

After you have your timeline completed, it is time to create a detailed budget. Use Figure 1. Budget tracker to ensure you capture all of the costs. This will allow you to see if the start up is feasible. A business is meant to grow, so starting out from your house is a great way to cut costs.

Step three:

Understand the tax advantages and consequences involved in your business. You should consult an accountant and review your business plan with them. Putting this effort in before you start investing your capital is essential. The more variables you remove from the equation, the easier the problem. These are the same steps you would use if you were presenting the business venture to a group of investors. With your money or someone else's money, it makes a great deal of sense to put substantial energy into the initial plan.

Step four:

Find a person that is successful in the business you are looking to start. Of course they have to be willing to sit down and talk with you. If the business owner does not want to invest time in talking with you, then do not waste any time and move on to the next person. Ideally, you will be able to show them your business plan and ask for their advice on it.

Step five:

Start your business. The idea of starting a new task or in this case a business can be intimidating. The planning and steps above should help to provide the confidence that you need for this challenge; then it is time to start the venture.

Remember that faith and persistence is required throughout the entire process. Entrust your plan and work to God, be positive, and work hard. The question is not if your resolve will be tested but rather when your resolve will be tested.

Final Thoughts

Are you living a weekly plan? I urge you to live a freedom plan. Integrate the leadership and financial concepts taught in this book regardless of your age and work toward your goals. When ever you approach a decision for that future 401K or real estate purchase, please refresh your memory on the topic by rereading that chapter. The investment of time to review the topic will yield the best decision for you. Finally, I personally believe that when you integrate God into your plan, amazing things will happen.

Recommended Reading List

In chapter two, I recommend reading in four areas. The four areas included religious, financial, leadership/relationship, and professional. I recommend reading the books in each category in the order listed. The order of the books in each category allows the reader to build their knowledge base while being exposed to different points of view. Remember that after completing a book in a category, move on to a book in a different category. Avoid reading two books in the same category consecutively. After getting in the habit of reading the Bible daily, I recommend reading the *The Magic of Thinking Big*, David Schwartz, PhD, to start the program. There isn't a time constraint associated with how long it should take you to complete each book; the key is what you take away from each author. One thing is for certain: reading will increase your knowledge base, allowing you to make more informed decisions.

Bible

I recommend you read daily.

Financial

1. *Rich Dad Poor Dad* by Robert Kiyosaki
2. *Morningstar Complete Investor* by Christine Benz and Pat Dorsey
3. *Overcoming Time Poverty* by Bill Quain, PhD
4. *Cash Flow Quadrant* by Robert Kiyosaki
5. *Ordinary People Extraordinary Wealth* by Ric Edelman
6. *One up on Wall Street* by Peter Lynch
7. *The Intelligent Investor* by Benjamin Graham, revised edition

Leadership and Relationship

1. *The Magic of Thinking Big* by David Schwartz, PhD
2. *Your Best Life Now* by Joel Osteen
3. *Personality Plus* by Florence Littauer

Professional

Be an expert in your profession; select a book or periodical to enhance your knowledge.

www.ingramcontent.com/pod-product-compliance
Lightning Source LLC
Chambersburg PA
CBHW022129170526
45157CB00004B/1809